A SPECTACULAR SEEK AND FIND CHALLENGE FOR ALL AGES!

BIGFOOT™
Goes Back in Time

D. L. MILLER

Happy Fox
BOOKS™

For Mom and Dad, and the Miller brothers who grew up in our little house nestled in the mountains of Western Maryland, where we spent many a day exploring the beauty and mysteries of the woods and creek bottoms just outside our front door.

— D. L. Miller

A Big Thank You

to all the BigFoot hunters around the world who not only believe that our big furry friend really does exist, but more importantly that he continues to inspire us to go outside and explore this great big world.

A Special Thank You

to the wonderful folks at Fox Chapel Publishing for bringing the BigFoot Seek and Find series to life, especially…

Publisher: Alan Giagnocavo
Vice President – Content: Christopher Reggio
Senior Editor: Laura Taylor
Managing Editor: Melissa Younger
Contributing Editors: Anthony Regolino, Jeremy Hauck, Katie Ocasio
Graphic Designer: David Fisk

© 2018 by D. L. Miller and Happy Fox Books, an imprint of Fox Chapel Publishing Company, Inc., 903 Square Street, Mount Joy, PA 17552.

Bigfoot Goes Back in Time is an original work, first published in 2018 by Fox Chapel Publishing Company, Inc.

ISBN 978-1-64124-003-1

Library of Congress Cataloging-in-Publication Data

Names: Miller, D. L. (David Lee), 1965- author.
Title: Bigfoot goes back in time / D.L. Miller.
Description: Mount Joy, PA : Happy Fox Books, [2018] | Audience: Ages 5-12.
Identifiers: LCCN 2018010342 | ISBN 9781641240031 (hardcover)
Subjects: LCSH: Sasquatch--Juvenile literature. | World history--Juvenile literature.
Classification: LCC QL89.2.S2 M5725 2018 | DDC 001.944--dc23
LC record available at https://lccn.loc.gov/2018010342

To learn more about the other great books from Fox Chapel Publishing, or to find a retailer near you, call toll-free 800-457-9112 or visit us at *www.FoxChapelPublishing.com*.

We are always looking for talented authors. To submit an idea, please send a brief inquiry to acquisitions@foxchapelpublishing.com.

Fox Chapel Publishing makes every effort to use environmentally friendly paper for printing.

Printed in China
First printing

Shutterstock images: Africa Studio (32 background; 33 background; 34 top left); Aggie 11 (30 dirt photos; 31 dirt photos); akedesign (20 background; 21 background); Andrey_Kuzmin (14 top left; 28 background; 29 background); andscha (42 top right); antoniomas (35 middle left); ArtMari (26 top left); Artur Balytskyi (22 top left); AVA Bitter (26 middle); AVprophoto (30 middle right); beodra (34 middle right); Boltenkoff (14 far right); Carso80 (39 top right); cosma (19 bottom left/center/right); Daniel Fung (42 top left); Danny Smythe (15 top center); Darios (30 middle left); Denise Kappa (26 bottom right); DnD-Production.com (35 bottom left); DR-images (43 top/middle/bottom left); DutchScenery (38 middle left); Edwin Verin (43 middle right); ESB Professional (18 top left); Everett Historical (18 middle left; 22 bottom left; 23 middle, top right; 30 top right; 31 upper middle right; 38 middle right, 39 top left, bottom right; 42 center left; 43 middle center); Evgeny Karandaev (24 background; 25 background); FlyBMW (34 top right); Fotokvadrat (14 top center); Fotovika (27 middle right); Gerald Bernard (27 bottom left); HelenField (44 background; 45 background); Henrik Lehnerer (42 middle right); ImagePost (36 background; 37 background); irin-k (40 background; 41 background); James R. Martin (38 bottom left); Jamie osborn (27 middle left); Janelle Lugge (31 top right); Jeff Bukowski (14 bottom left); jennyt (39 bottom left); jgorzynik (27 top right); josefauer (31 lower middle right); Kelvin Degree (30 top left); Konoplin Dmitriy (14 middle center); Lipskiy (27 bottom right); MatiasDelCarmine (15 top right); Michael Rosskothen (22 top right); michelaubryphoto (19 top/middle/bottom left); Milkovasa (19 far right); Mjosedesign (39 top right, middle center); morisfoto (26 bottom left); Nejron Photo (14 top left); Nerthuz (43 bottom right); Nicku (22 top right); nikkytok (42 bottom background); optimarc (31 bottom right); Ortis (34 middle left; 35 rope photos); Pablo77 (15 bottom left); paulinux (38 top right); Peter Lorimer (15 top left/center/right); photo one (30 bottom right); photosoft (12 background; 13 background); RachelKolokoffHopper (34 bottom background); REDPIXEL.PL (30 bottom left); RetroClipArt (27 top left); Samet Guler (18 bottom background); seecreateimages (43 background); sloukam (19 middle center); Songsak P (35 middle right); spatuletail (31 upper middle right); Steve Cukrov (35 bottom right); travelview (23 bottom right); valzan (31 lower middle center); Victorian Traditions (35 top right); Vladimir Wrangel (19 top left); XEG (14 bottom right); Zimneva Natalia (15 middle)

BiGFOOT CONTENTS

Are you ready to walk with dinosaurs, explore a castle, and pan for gold?
BigFoot takes a trip back in time and you get to come along and join the adventure!

HOW TO USE THIS BOOK

Read a bit about each time period.
You may learn something surprising!

Turn the page and search for BigFoot. The keys along
the sides tell you what else to look for. Good luck!

WHO IS BIGFOOT?

Stories about BigFoot have been around for years in many countries. Some people believe he's a **giant bear** that walks around on two legs. Other people think he may be a **giant gorilla** roaming the forests.

WARNING
BIGFOOT AREA
STAY ON MARKED TRAILS

This picture is from the famous **Patterson-Gimlin film**, taken in 1967 in Northern California's **Six Rivers National Forest** by Roger Patterson and Bob Gimlin. Some people think this is just a person in a costume. Others believe it's the real **BigFoot**. What do you think?

BIG FOOT XING

DUE TO SIGHTINGS IN THE AREA OF A CREATURE RESEMBLING "BIG FOOT" THIS SIGN HAS BEEN POSTED FOR YOUR SAFETY

HAVE YOU SEEN A REAL BIGFOOT?

There are different stories about what the giant, furry creature looks like. But they all share some details: a big, human-like creature standing **7 feet (2.3 m) to 9 feet (3 m) tall**. BigFoot is brown, but many have also seen black, gray, white, and greenish-blue BigFoots. Some say that he has **large eyes** and a large forehead. The top of his head is like the shape of a large gorilla. If you see someone walking around that looks like this, you're probably looking at BigFoot!

BigFoot might be able to run up to 30 miles per hour (48 kph)—twice as fast as a person!

WHERE DID THE NAME BIGFOOT COME FROM?

In the 1800s, the name *BigFoot* was used for huge **grizzly bears** that were seen in parts of the United States. Some believe that **David Thompson**, a man crossing the Rocky Mountains in the winter of 1811, saw the first real BigFoot footprints in the snow. The tracks were too big for even the **largest bear**. The name was again used when people started seeing **huge footprints** in the forest that looked bigger than a large bear's. These footprints were about 24 inches (61 cm) long and 8 inches (20 cm) wide, **twice as big** as an adult shoe. Many people believe that these big footprints are enough proof that our BigFoot **really does exist!**

BiGFOOT GOES BY MANY NAMES

BigFoot has many names around the world, including the most common: **Sasquatch.**
So don't forget to tell people you're going **"Squatching"** the next time you decide to search for our giant, furry friend. What do other parts of the world call BigFoot?

Barmanou (Pakistan)

Basajuan (Spain)

Big Greyman (Scotland)

Gin-Sung (China)

Hibagon (Japan)

Kapre (Philippines)

Kushtaka (Alaska, USA)

Mapinguari (Brazil and Bolivia)

Menk (Russia)

Moehau (New Zealand)

Mogollon Monster (Arizona, USA)

Orange Pendek (Indonesia)

Skunk Ape (Florida, USA)

Ucu (Argentina)

Waterbobbejaan (South Africa)

Wendigo (Canada)

Woodwosa (England)

Yeren (Mongolia)

Yeti (Russia)

Yowie (Australia)

Dinosaurs

Microraptor

ALL SHAPES AND SIZES

Dinosaurs were reptiles that lived between 245 million and 66 million years ago during the **Mesozoic Era**. Some dinosaurs were as small as chickens (**Microraptor**) and some were as tall as a 7-story building (**Argentinosaurus**). Even BigFoot would look small compared to some of these supersized animals!

There were over **1,000 kinds** of dinosaurs!

Argentinosaurus

MIGHTY MESOZOIC ERA

The Mesozoic Era is divided into three time periods: **Triassic** (252–201 million years ago), **Jurassic** (201–145 million years ago), and **Cretaceous** (145–66 million years ago).

The word **dinosaur** comes from the Greek words **deinos** (meaning "awesome" or "fearfully great") plus **sauros** ("lizard"). So, "awesome lizard"!

The biggest carnivorous dinosaur–Spinosaurus–lived in Africa! BigFoot has seen some of today's wildest animals in Africa (*BigFoot Goes on Vacation*).

BIGFOOT *Goes On Vacation*

The biggest dinosaur eggs were the size of basketballs.

The longest name for a dinosaur is Micropachycephalosaurus. Say that 10 times fast!

DiG iT!

The study of dinosaurs is called **paleontology**, and paleontologists search for fossils all over the world. **Fossils** are very old plant and animal material that has been buried in the ground for millions of years. Paleontologists get to dig in the dirt to look for **dinosaur bones**!

AND THEN THEY WERE GONE . . .

All dinosaur life ended suddenly and mysteriously **66 million years ago**. Most scientists believe that some kind of huge event—like an **asteroid crash** or **volcanic eruptions**—changed the Earth's environment and made it impossible for dinosaurs to survive.

Some dinosaurs were meat eaters (carnivores), but most were plant eaters (herbivores). The largest herbivores had to eat 2,000 pounds (907 kg) of plants each day. That's like a bus-sized pile of veggies!

A stegosaurus had a body the size of a van and a brain the size of a walnut.

Most dinosaurs had tails to help them keep their balance. Some tails were 45 feet (14 m) long—nearly the length of a tractor-trailer!

THE FiERCE T-REX

🦶 **Teeth** were 6–12 inches (15–30 cm) long.

🦶 Could eat around **500 pounds** (230 kg) of meat in **one bite**!

🦶 **Front legs** were about the size of human arms, and they were **too short to reach its mouth**.

6 Galloping Yellow Iguanodons

9 Dancing Allosauruses

9 Spiky Tail Stegosauruses

6 Pterodactyls with Tails

8 Bumbling Brachiosauruses

ICE AGE

BRRRRRRRR!

An ice age is when the temperature drops and huge areas of land are covered in—you guessed it!—**ice**. The last ice age happened around 20,000 years ago. That's when **glaciers** (sheets of ice that slowly move) created ice "bridges" that connected continents. Using these bridges, people and animals went from **Africa** to **Europe** and **Asia**.

A bear from the Ice Age called Arctodus weighed about 2 tons and could stand up to 13 feet (4 m) tall. Could this bear be BigFoot's distant cousin?

BigFoot was very cold after visiting the Ice Age! See if you can find him warming up at the beach in *BigFoot Goes on Vacation*.

GOT ICE?

The ice age is not gone forever! The Earth experiences global ice covering about every **100,000 years**, when the Earth's orbit moves farther away from the sun. We now have only two ice sheets on Earth: **Greenland** and **Antarctica**, the largest. Antarctica's ice sheet measures up to 4 miles (6 km) thick and contains **7.2 million cubic miles** (30 million cubic km) of frozen water!

5

There have been 5 ice ages throughout Earth's history.

TIGERS, MAMMOTHS & CAMELOPS, OH MY!

Many animals from the last ice age are **extinct** due to climate change and hunting by humans. The **saber-toothed tiger** had upper canine teeth that measured 7 inches (18 cm) long. **Woolly mammoths** were the same size as today's African elephants, but the mammoth had long hair and tusks that were about 15 feet (5 m) long. North American camels—called "**camelops**"—were actually more like **llamas**. They were about 7 feet (2 m) tall and weighed up to 1,800 pounds (800 kg).

In the ice age, giant ground sloths were about 10 feet (3 m) long and weighed over a ton.

Today's sloth only grows to 2 feet (.6 m) long!

As glaciers move, they carve deep valleys in the land.

5 Giant Gray Slow-Moving Armadillos

8 Snarling Saber-Toothed Tigers

7 Sniffing Short-Faced Bears

7 Darling Dire Wolves

7 Giant Ground Sloths

VIKINGS

WARRIOR EXPLORERS

The Vikings came from **Norway**, **Sweden**, and **Denmark** and were powerful from the 800s until 1100 CE. The name "Viking" comes from a language called Old Norse and means **"a pirate raid."** Vikings traveled by sea, often to conquer other people and take their food, weapons, and riches. Led by explorer **Leif Eriksson**, they visited North America nearly 500 years before Columbus did.

Sculpture of Leif Eriksson

Viking ships were hard work to sail. Sometimes BigFoot likes to relax and have fun on a cruise! (*BigFoot Goes on Vacation*)

Vikings are still a symbol of strength today, especially in football-loving, icy-cold Minnesota!

THE REAL DEAL

Unlike how they were shown in old paintings and operas—and on football helmets today!—real **Viking helmets** did not have horns on them. **Horns** on a helmet just weren't practical. They would make it too easy to get stuck in a low tree branch during a **battle**!

14

While rowing, Vikings may have sat on their sea chests—wooden boxes that held their belongings.

VIKING FUN

Vikings liked telling **epic stories** about heroes and gods. They really liked **wrestling, tug-of-war**, and board games like **chess**. Vikings also skied for sport and as a way to get around their snowy homeland.

GOING BERSERK?

Today the English word **berserk** means "crazy." It came from the Old Norse word **berserkr**, the name of Viking warriors who wore animal skins and howled like animals during battle.

SHIPBUILDING

Viking ships were made of **wooden planks**, usually from oak trees. The side planks of the ship were overlapped, making the ship very sturdy. **Wooden pegs** and **iron rivets** held the planks together. To make the ship waterproof, animal wool and tar from pine trees was placed in every joint. The ship had sails made from woven wool. The **Vikings** rowed with long wooden oars. One man steered the ship from the back (stern) using a big steering oar.

DANGEROUS DRAKKARS

A **Drakkar** was a fast Viking **longship** that had a **dragon** or serpent head carved on the front (prow) to strike fear in those who saw them coming. A Drakkar had a crew of **25–60** men—some larger ones could carry **100**—who rowed, ate, and slept on the deck. There was some space below deck for supplies. Viking sailors used the sun to find their way: they knew the sunrise was east and the sunset was west. At night they watched the stars to **navigate**. They could sail on seas as well as go on rivers and streams.

1 BigFoot

1 Legendary Footprint

5 Viking Boats with Red and Purple Sails

6 Cawing Ravens

9 Curious Whales with Heads above the Water

6 Floating Oars

9 Silly Sea Serpents

14 Soaring Seagulls

7 Vikings on Lookout

MEDIEVAL CASTLE

These old castles are a lot bigger than what you might see at Mini-Golf World! (BigFoot Goes on Vacation)

MANY NAMES, ONE TIME

Beginning in the 400s and lasting until the 1400s, the **Medieval Era** is also known as the **Dark Ages**. It was called "dark" because people used to think nothing new had been done in art, science, math, or music. But plenty of new things were first used during this time, such as gunpowder, mechanical clocks, and eyeglasses. The first mechanical printing press was built by **Johannes Gutenberg** in **1450** in Germany. This era was also called the Age of Faith due to the spread of Christianity and Islam throughout the world.

Johannes Gutenberg and his press

There are 1,500 castle sites in England.

HOME SWEET CASTLE

Medieval castles were used as both a palace home for a king and a fort to defend against invaders. The main room in the castle was the **great hall** where the king had meetings and held big feasts with entertainment by jugglers and singers. Castles often had a **moat**—a wide ditch with water to keep invaders from getting inside. When prisoners were captured during war, they were locked up in the castle's **underground dungeon**.

Spiral staircases were used in castles to make it hard for invaders to use their weapons in that tight space.

A GOOD KNIGHT

Knights were rich soldiers in the Medieval Era who wore armor and fought on horseback. The road to knighthood began in childhood: a young boy became a knight's page (servant) at the age of 7, then a **squire** (apprentice) by the age of 15. When the squire turned 21, he became a knight and spent his time away at war, training for war, or doing tournaments and **jousting**. By the end of the Medieval Era, knights were no longer needed. Countries had armies with plenty of soldiers, and war had changed so that the clunky armor was useless against new guns.

Most early castles were made with wood, and some of them lasted for 400—500 years.

There are still knights today, but none of them wear armor! Kings and queens make people knights to honor them for something special they've done for their country.

It took about 10 years to build a castle.

Castles weren't built much after the Medieval Era, since new, powerful cannons could destroy a castle's stone walls.

WINDSOR CASTLE

Many **medieval castles** were destroyed during war or left to fall apart over time. Some that survived were turned into **monuments** for tourists to visit. Other surviving castles are still used by the same families who lived there many years ago. The oldest castle that people still live in is Windsor Castle. It is now the home of **Queen Elizabeth II** of England. It was built in the **1000s** and was made mostly from wood. **King Henry I** lived there in the early 1100s. He wanted it to always be the home of English kings and queens. Over time it was rebuilt with stone and made bigger until it became the beautiful castle it is today.

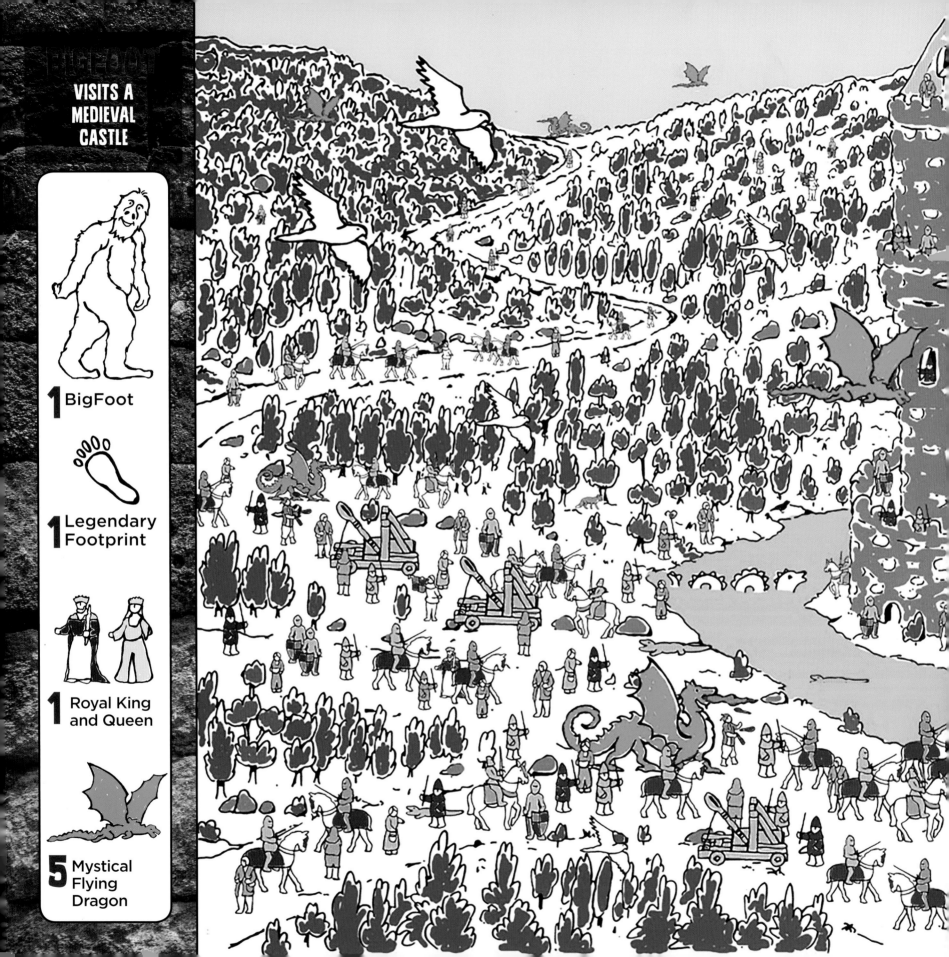

1 BigFoot

1 Legendary
Footprint

1 Royal King
and Queen

5 Mystical
Flying
Dragon

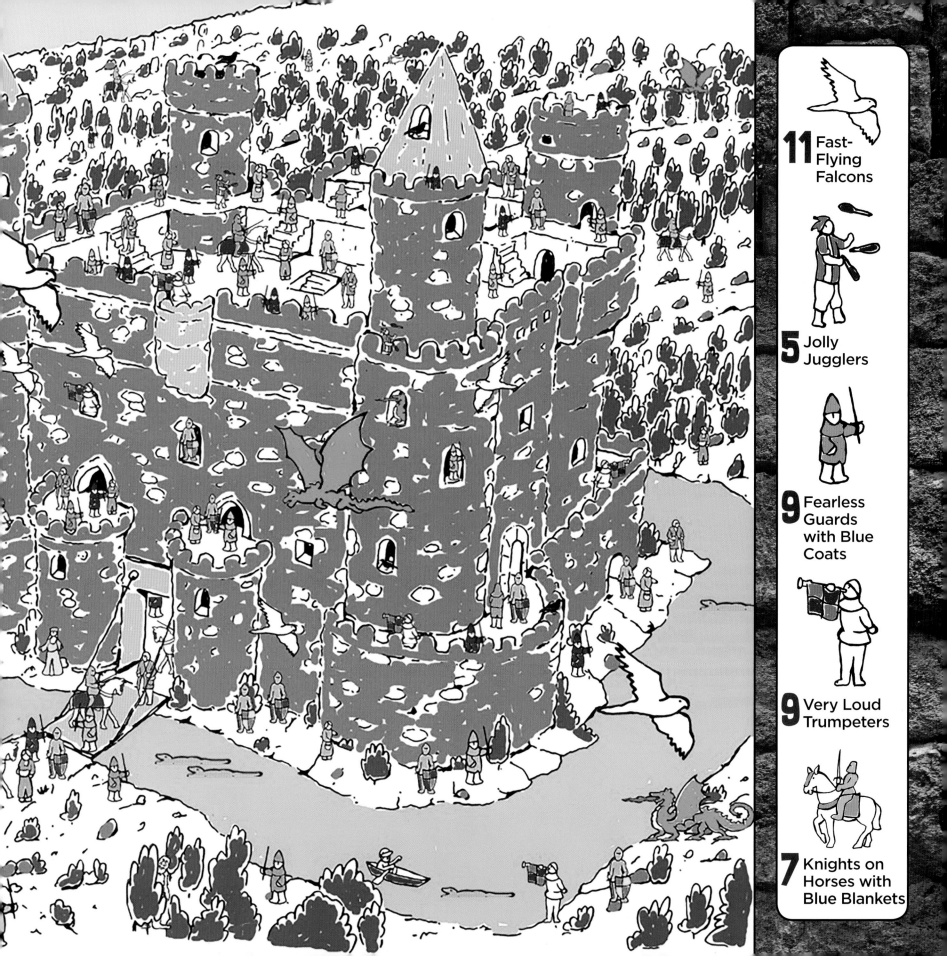

AIRSHIPS

BALLOON ANIMALS

The first hot-air balloon passengers weren't people! On September 19, 1783, in France, a **duck**, a **rooster**, and a **sheep** rode in a hot-air balloon built by brothers Joseph-Michel and Jacques Étienne Montgolfier. The balloon flew about 2 miles (3.2 km) in 8 minutes and then **safely landed**. Over 130,000 people watched this historic animal flight!

UP, UP, AND AWAY

The first hot-air balloon flight with two men aboard took place on November 21, 1783, in Paris, France. The balloon flew about **5.5 miles** (9 km) in 25 minutes. **Benjamin Franklin** was there and wrote about it in his journal: "We could not help feeling a certain mixture of awe and admiration."

BigFoot saw a lot of giant, colorful hot-air balloons when he joined a balloon festival in *BigFoot Goes on Vacation*!

Montgolfiers Luftballoon, 1783.

SPY SHIPS

Long before anyone could imagine that the military would have its own **Air Force**, hot-air balloons were used during war to find enemies. The **French** were the first to use hot-air balloons this way, forming the French **Aerostatic Corps** in 1794.

In the American Civil War (1861-1865), Union soldiers flew in hot-air balloons to spy on Confederate troops.

ZEPPELIN

Ferdinand von Zeppelin learned about airships when he visited the United States during the Civil War and saw how hot-air balloons were used. When he returned to **Germany**, he started a company that made airships to carry people. The company and its famous airships were named after him.

Airships (or "dirigibles") flew only a few hundred feet above the ground.

Dining room of the Hindenburg, 1936.

Hindenburg airship being built at the Zeppelin Company in Germany (1931–1936).

CROSSING THE ATLANTIC

In the early 1900s, airships had **metal frames** for greater support and strength. They could fly from America to Germany without running out of fuel. In the 1920s and 1930s, the airship **Graf Zeppelin** could fly **20 passengers** plus crew members from Lakehurst, New Jersey, to Friedrichshafen, Germany, in about 3 days. Cruise ships of the time took about **6 days** to sail across the Atlantic Ocean. Today, an airplane ride from Germany to America takes only 9 hours!

GOOD YEAR

GLIMPSE A BLIMP

Airships that do not have **metal frames** are called **blimps**. They will lose their shape unless they're filled with gas, usually helium. The **Goodyear Tire & Rubber Company** has used blimps to advertise its products since 1925. Today its designs are not technically blimps but semi-rigid airships. Look for the Goodyear "blimp" when you're watching a big football game on TV: the blimp provides overhead shots from its **onboard camera**.

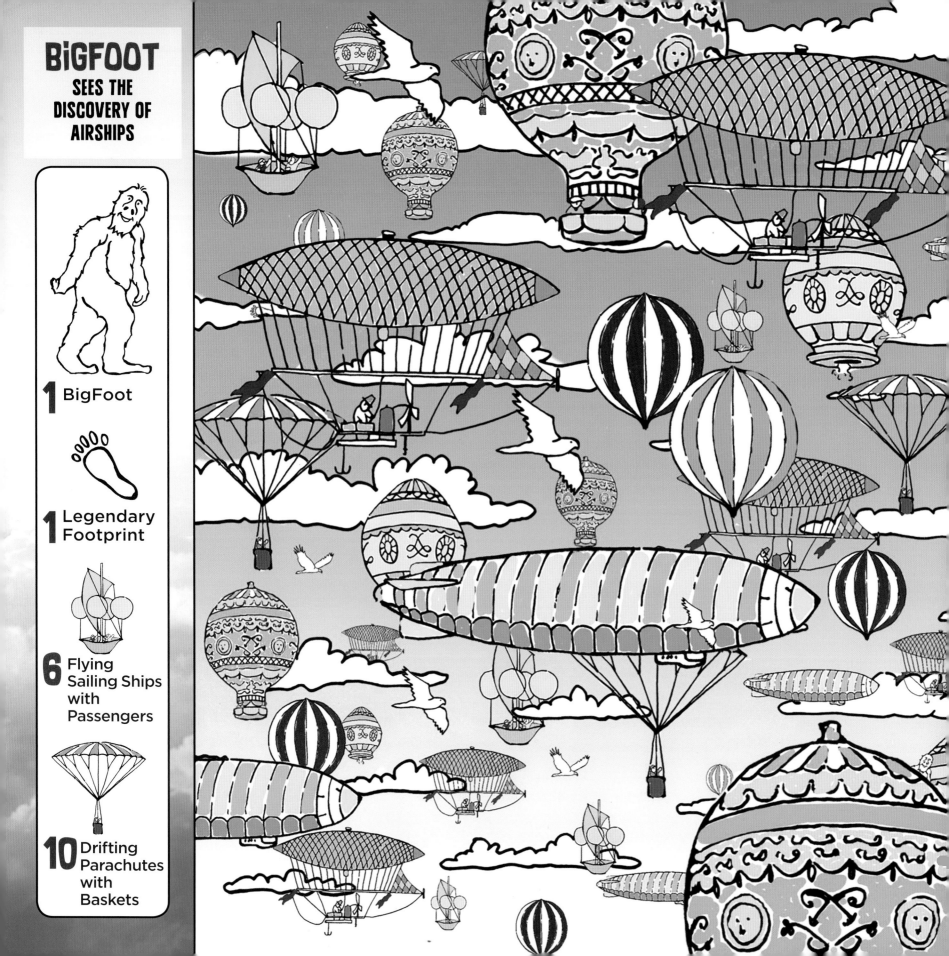

BiGFOOT
SEES THE DISCOVERY OF AIRSHIPS

1 BigFoot

1 Legendary Footprint

6 Flying Sailing Ships with Passengers

10 Drifting Parachutes with Baskets

7 Green and White Floating Balloons

9 Massive Dirigibles

10 Lighter-Than-Air Floating Machines

12 Super Steam-Powered Airships

11 Smoke-Filled Balloons

STEAM ENGINE

The fastest train in the world is in Shanghai, China, and goes 267 mph (431 kph).

PARTS OF A STEAM LOCOMOTIVE

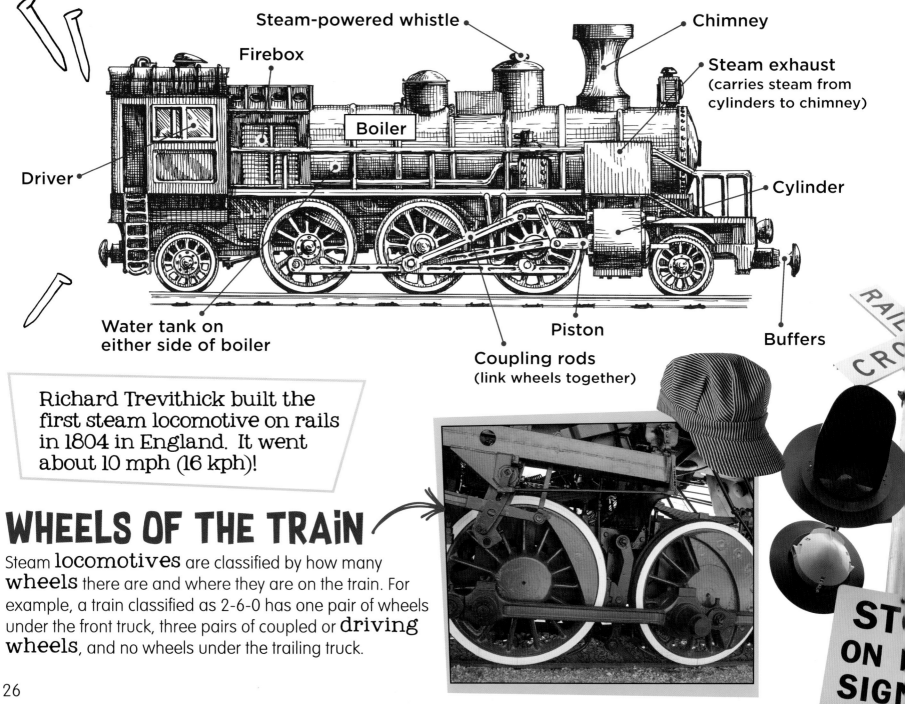

Steam-powered whistle

Chimney

Firebox

Steam exhaust
(carries steam from
cylinders to chimney)

Boiler

Driver

Cylinder

Water tank on
either side of boiler

Piston

Buffers

Coupling rods
(link wheels together)

Richard Trevithick built the first steam locomotive on rails in 1804 in England. It went about 10 mph (16 kph)!

WHEELS OF THE TRAIN

Steam locomotives are classified by how many wheels there are and where they are on the train. For example, a train classified as 2-6-0 has one pair of wheels under the front truck, three pairs of coupled or driving wheels, and no wheels under the trailing truck.

RAIL
CRO

ST
ON
SIGN

ALL ABOARD!

From the mid-1800s to the early 1900s, **steam locomotives** were used around the world. Each one needed a crew of three people to drive it. The **conductor** made sure all the passengers were on board, then told the **engineer** when it was time to go. The engineer told the **fireman** when it was time to add more coal to the firebox in the engine. The engineer also watched the tracks for anything in the way.

The smoke coming out of a steam locomotive's chimney is a mix of coal smoke and steam.

STEAM POWER

How does steam make a huge train move? By burning coal to **1400°F** (760°C), the fire box heats the water tank next to it to boiling temperature. The boiling water creates **steam**. The steam builds up in **pressure** and makes the pistons move. The **pistons** are connected to **rods**, and the rods are attached to wheels. So when the pistons move, so do the rods and wheels, and the train moves forward.

In 1830, there were only 23 miles (37 km) of railroad track in the United States. By 1916, there were 250,000 miles (402,300 km) of track—enough to reach the moon from Earth.

TRAIN VS. HORSE

America's **first** steam locomotive lost a race with a horse! On **August 28, 1830**, Peter Cooper's "Tom Thumb" engine raced against a horse-drawn train on tracks near **Baltimore, Maryland**. The steam engine was winning but then a mechanical problem forced the engine to quit, and the horse won the race.

Steam engines were used in trains, ships (including the *Titanic*), and even some early cars.

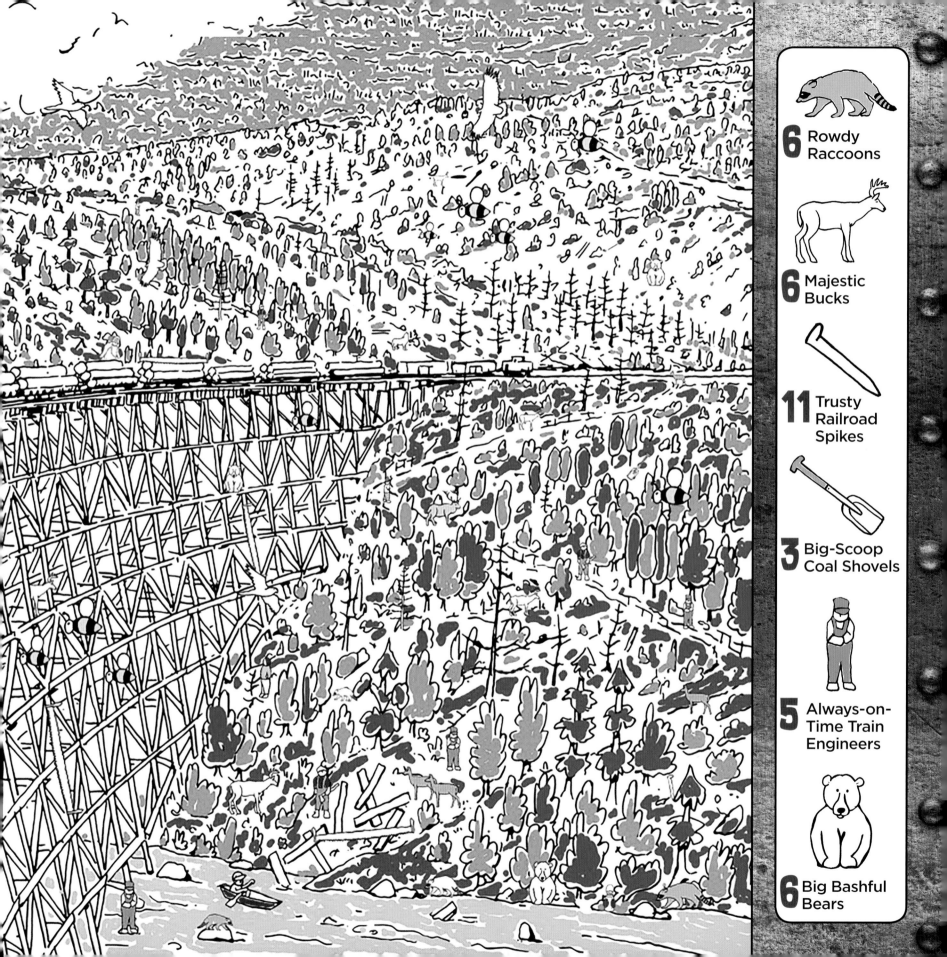

6 Rowdy Raccoons

6 Majestic Bucks

11 Trusty Railroad Spikes

3 Big-Scoop Coal Shovels

5 Always-on-Time Train Engineers

6 Big Bashful Bears

GOLD RUSH

GOLDEN DREAMS

On **January 24, 1848**, when a carpenter named James Marshall was building a sawmill for John Sutter on the American River near Coloma, California, he discovered **gold flecks** shining in the water. Despite Sutter and Marshall's best efforts to keep the gold a secret, word got out. Men from around the world left their homes to search for **gold**. While some did find it, most of them worked long days with no gold in sight and had to find other work.

PANNING FOR GOLD

Early miners searched rivers for **gold nuggets**. With a circular metal pan, they scooped up some sand, pebbles, and water from the riverbed. Then they **shook** the pan, letting some of the water and sand spill out. The heavier gold would sink to the bottom of the pan. **Panning** was slow, hard work while standing in cold water, bent over searching for gold.

GOOD BUSINESS

There was usually more money to be made by selling supplies to miners than there was in trying to find gold. **Levi Strauss**, for example, started selling denim pants in a San Francisco store in **1850**, and Henry Wells and William Fargo opened a bank in town. Future carmaker John Studebaker got rich selling wheelbarrows to gold miners.

Gold miners started arriving in California in 1849, so they were called '49ers.

BOOMTOWNS

Small, quiet towns that quickly became busy little cities were called **boomtowns**. They were filled with gold miners and the businesses to support them (like hotels, stores, saloons, banks, and stables). When miners couldn't find any more gold and left the area, many boomtowns were deserted. Then they were called **ghost towns**.

Ghost town of Bodie, CO

San Francisco, 1851

PERMANENT IMPACT

While the Gold Rush didn't last too long (1849–1856), it changed the United States forever. Before the Gold Rush, the West was mostly unsettled frontier land. Then in 1849, nearly **100,000 people** moved to California!

FROM GOLD TO GRAPES

By **1856**, mining for gold was just a regular job in mines owned by big companies; the rush was over in California. But the state's farms were really growing! **Crops** like grapes, almonds, pistachios, olives, pomegranates, lemons, and avocados still bring the state a lot of business today.

To "hit pay dirt" meant to find dirt filled with gold.

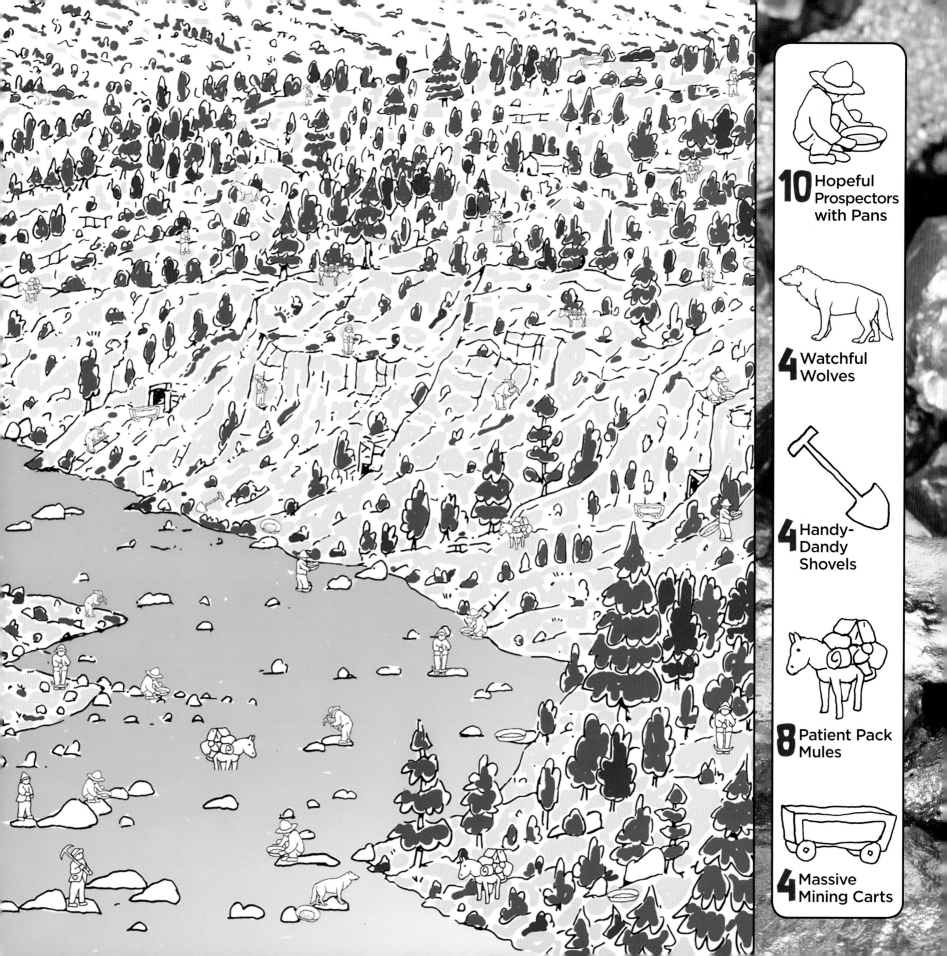

10 Hopeful Prospectors with Pans

4 Watchful Wolves

4 Handy-Dandy Shovels

8 Patient Pack Mules

4 Massive Mining Carts

CATTLE DRIVE

COWS COULD DRIVE?

No, cows didn't drive! A "cattle drive" was when **cowboys** moved a large herd of cows and bulls from one place to another by guiding—or "**driving**"—them along a trail.

Texas Longhorns were the breed usually found on cattle drives.

There are around 99 million cattle in the USA today!

FREE ROAMING

Free-range **cattle herding** was brought to the United States by vaqueros (cowboys) from Mexico in the 1800s. Ranchers **branded(marked)** their cattle and let the animals roam free and graze on the open range. There were **no fences**. When it was time to herd the animals together, the cowboys could easily find their cattle by the brand.

A ranch is a large farm for raising horses, sheep, or beef cattle.

PLENTY OF LAND

The **Wild West** was an untamed, lawless place. From about **1865 to 1895**, it was the area of the United States that was west of the Mississippi River. Life there was dangerous and had few towns and sheriffs, so why did people want to go? **Land!** There was a lot of it that could be used to grow crops and raise cattle.

WAGON TRAILS

In the early **1800s**, traders and fur trappers made the **Oregon** and **Santa Fe Trails**. They both started in Independence, Missouri. The Oregon Trail is famous for the covered wagons that carried everything settlers owned on the **2,000-mile** (3,219-km) trip to Oregon City. The Santa Fe Trail was mostly used for trade to New Mexico. It was 900 miles (1,448 km) long.

"Chuck" was a slang term for food.

NOT-SO-FAST FOOD

When **cowboys** were on a cattle drive, a **chuck wagon** (a covered wagon filled with food and cooking gear) went with them. A **cook** was hired to drive the wagon and make all of the **meals**. A meal was beef or salt pork, potatoes, beans, gravy, sourdough biscuits, and coffee. There were no fresh vegetables or fruit. The wagon did have a water barrel. The cook was called **"cookie"** in cowboy slang. As keeper of the food, he was a very important person on the cattle drive!

35

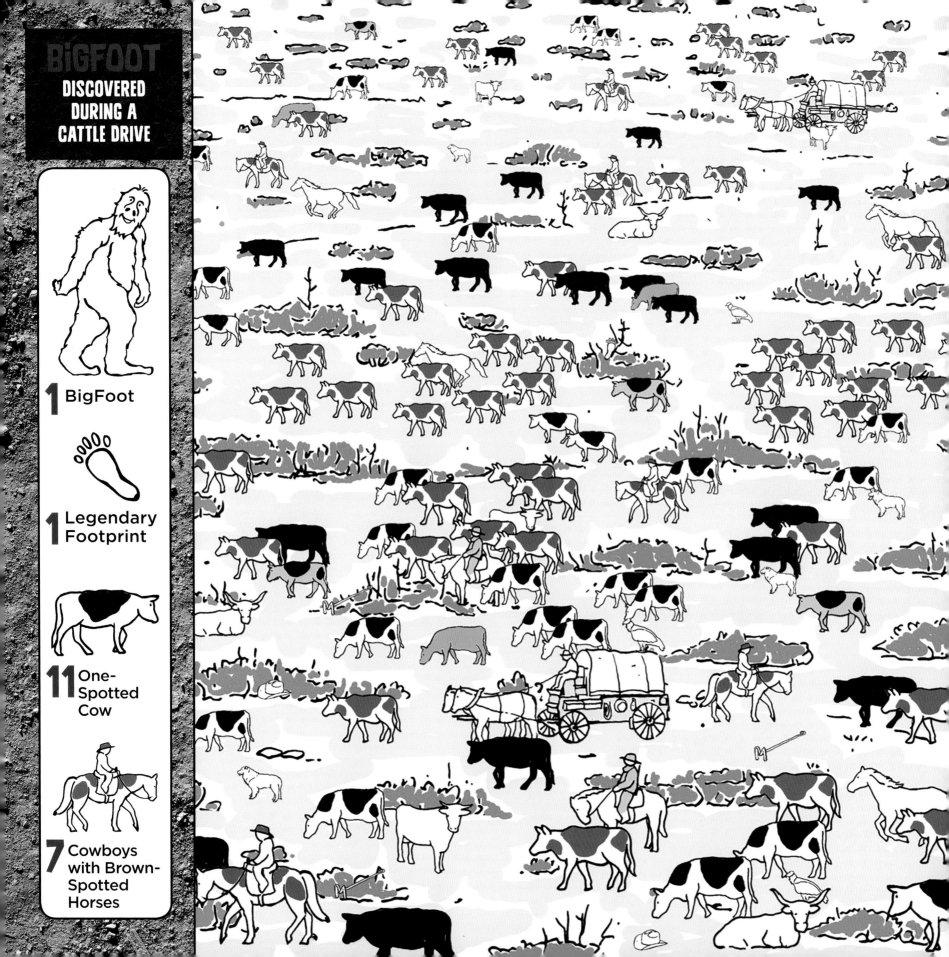

BiGFOOT

DISCOVERED
DURING A
CATTLE DRIVE

1 BigFoot

1 Legendary
Footprint

11 One-
Spotted
Cow

7 Cowboys
with Brown-
Spotted
Horses

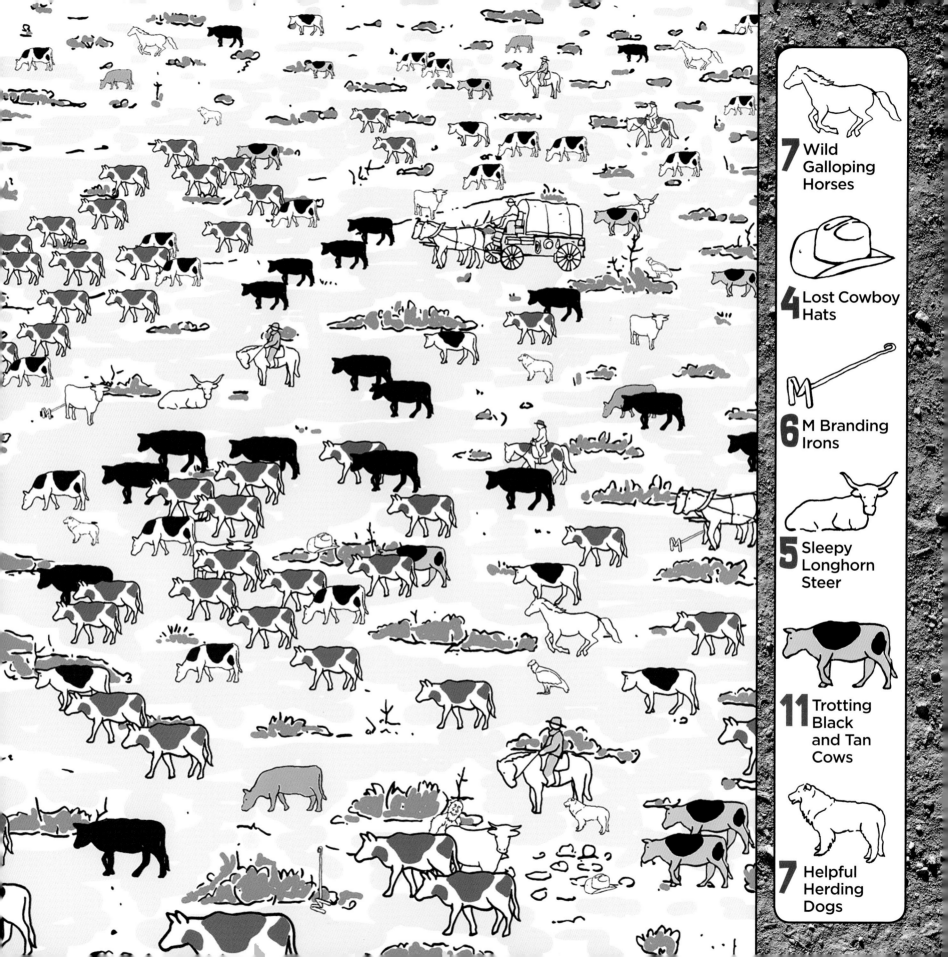

7 Wild Galloping Horses

4 Lost Cowboy Hats

6 M Branding Irons

5 Sleepy Longhorn Steer

11 Trotting Black and Tan Cows

7 Helpful Herding Dogs

First Flights

Wilbur Wright 1867-1912

Orville Wright 1871-1948

iT ALL STARTED WiTH A TOY

In 1878 when **Wilbur** and **Orville Wright** were young boys, their father brought home a model helicopter based on a design by French aviation pioneer **Alphonse Penaud**. The boys loved the toy. This was the beginning of their love of flying.

Bicycles and airplanes are similar: both need balance and control, an aerodynamic shape, and a lightweight but sturdy body.

Otto Lilienthal

RESEARCH FiRST

The Wright brothers' study of flight started with learning about other flights. They were really interested in the work of German aviator **Otto Lilienthal**. He was the first person to make successful gliding flights in the late **1800s**.

BiKES TO PLANES

In **1892**, the Wright brothers opened their bicycle repair shop called the **Wright Cycle Company** in Dayton, Ohio. Wilbur and Orville decided to build and sell their own bicycle in 1895. They earned enough money for their airplane experiments. Building bikes also helped them understand how to build an airplane.

Wilbur was born on April 16, 1867, and Orville was born on August 19, 1871.

WRIGHT CYCLE CO.

AiRBORNE!

The Wright brothers picked **Kitty Hawk**, North Carolina, as the place to try flying a plane because the strong winds there would help their liftoff. On **December 17, 1903**, Wilbur succeeded in the first controlled, power-driven flight for almost a minute. He flew 852 feet (260 m) high in their airplane called the **Flyer**.

WILBUR AND ORVILLE WRIGHT

FAMOUS FOR FLiGHT

Wilbur and Orville met many American journalists and scientists who didn't believe they had flown a plane. In **1908**, Wilbur went to **France** and found that people there were more willing to believe him. He even met with royalty and government officials to talk about his flight. Orville joined his brother in 1909. The pair sold many of their planes in Europe. Then they went back to the United States, where they finally got the credit they were due.

REPLiCA OF THE FLYER

The Wright brothers' **Flyer** looked nothing like what you think of when someone says the word **airplane** today. Unlike the giant aluminum planes we have now, the **Flyer** was more of a glider with an engine. It had double wings and was made mostly from the wood of spruce and ash trees.

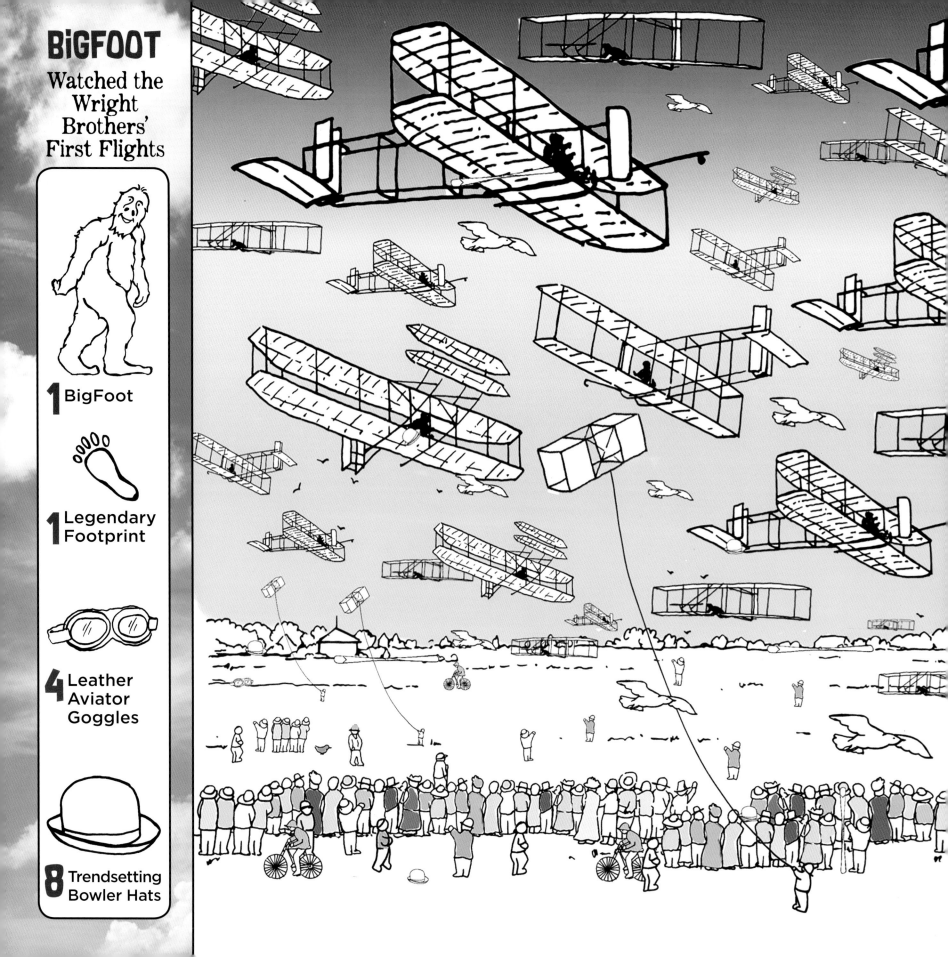

BiGFOOT
Watched the Wright Brothers' First Flights

1 BigFoot

1 Legendary Footprint

4 Leather Aviator Goggles

8 Trendsetting Bowler Hats

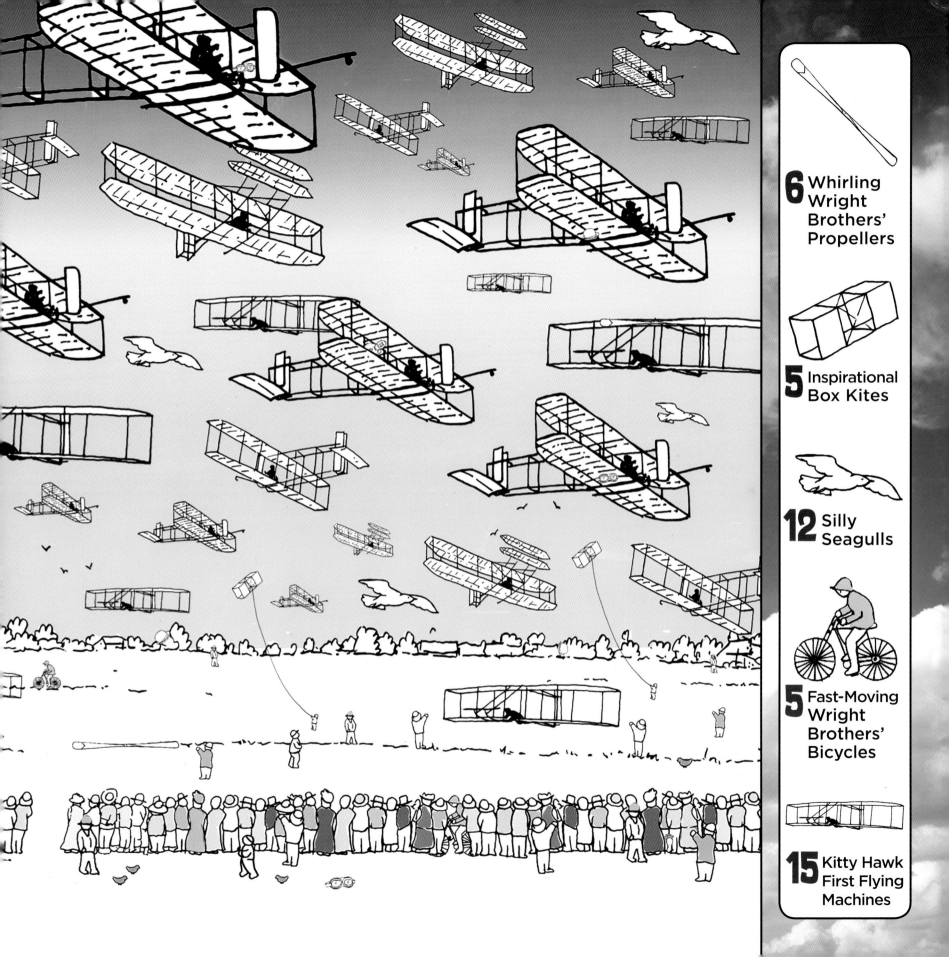

6 Whirling Wright Brothers' Propellers

5 Inspirational Box Kites

12 Silly Seagulls

5 Fast-Moving Wright Brothers' Bicycles

15 Kitty Hawk First Flying Machines

Moon Walks

MOON WALKERS

Twelve men have walked on the moon. These twelve men—all Americans—are still the only human beings to have walked on any planetary body other than Earth. Ever. Maybe in the future men and women will follow in their **footsteps** on the moon or maybe somewhere else in a galaxy far, far away. . . .

A SPECTACULAR SEEK AND FIND CHALLENGE FOR ALL AGES!

BiGFOOT Goes On Vacation

Along with flying high into space, BigFoot has also been seen diving deep into the ocean (*BigFoot Goes on Vacation*).

"That's one small step for man, one giant leap for mankind."

-Neil Armstrong, July 20, 1969, speaking the first words on the moon

ARE WE THERE YET?

The moon is **239,000 miles** (385,000 km) away from Earth—about a **3-day trip** in an Apollo spacecraft. That's like driving from New York to Los Angeles (2,790 miles [4,490 km]) 86 times. Makes that family road trip seem pretty short!

MOON TIME

Alan Shepard walked on the moon for over 9 hours. David Scott and Jim Irwin drove around in a moon buggy for 14 hours. But NASA saved the best for last. **Apollo 17** astronauts Gene Cernan and Jack Schmitt spent the most time in the lunar great outdoors. Over 3 days, they made **3 moon walks**. They only went in their lunar module at night to sleep.

NASA stands for National Aeronautics and Space Administration.

In the summer of 1969, over 600 million people watched TV to see Neil Armstrong step out of his lunar module.

WHAT HAPPENED TO APOLLO 13?

On **April 13, 1970**, Apollo 13 was only **40,000 miles** (64,000 km) away from the moon. The astronauts inside were ready to go exploring. But then a **spark** caused one of the spacecraft's oxygen tanks to explode. The moon landing was canceled, and their new mission was to survive. The astronauts shut down as many systems as possible to save power and oxygen. After a wild, uncomfortable ride back to Earth, Apollo 13 landed safely in the **Pacific Ocean**.

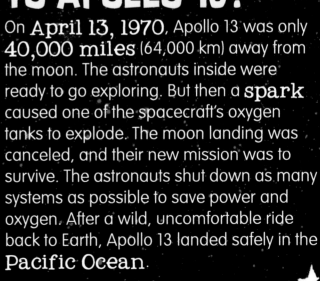

BiGFOOT

SPOTTED
DURING
MOON WALKS

1 BigFoot

1 Legendary Footprint

14 Must-Have Moon Rocks

5 Lumbering Lunar Rovers with Astronauts

13 World-Famous Moon Walk Footprints

12 Slow-Moving Moon Walkers

8 Cosmic Command Service Modules

6 Spunky Sputnik Satellites

4 Tasty Moon Pies

ANSWER KEY

Even in places far back in time, BigFoot is an expert at staying lost. He climbs roofs, hides behind buildings, blends into crowds—it's tricky work finding him! If you were stumped the first time around, you can use this guide—the **small red dot** shows where his elusive footprint is, while the **big red dot** in each picture reveals BigFoot himself. Just as in real life, the people, animals, and objects are easier to spot than finding BigFoot, so they are not included in this answer key.

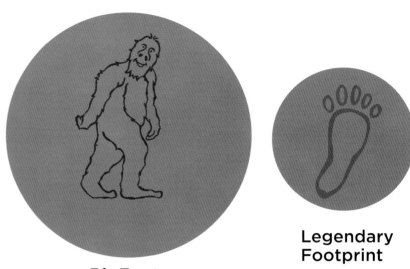

BigFoot

Legendary Footprint

Dinosaurs

Ice Age

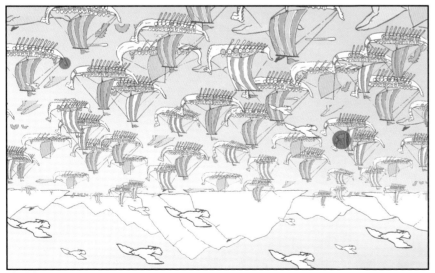

Vikings

Medieval Castle

Airships

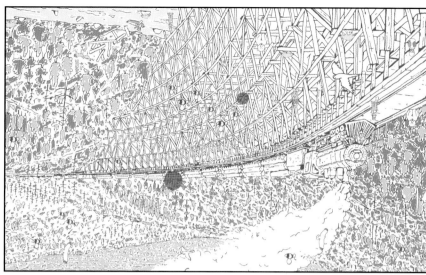

Steam Engine

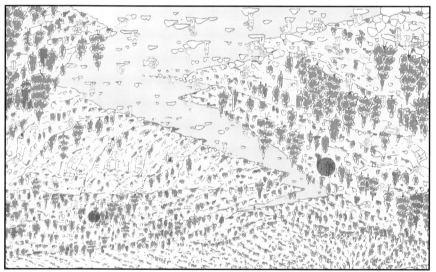

Gold Rush

Cattle Drive

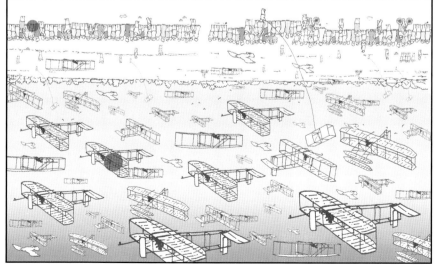

First Flights

Moon Walks

ABOUT THE ARTIST

As with BigFoot, the artist and creator of this series is a bit on the elusive side. He is rarely seen in public, spending most of his days sketching in his studio located among the mighty oak trees found only in the deep, dark woods far off the beaten path.

Deeply inspired by nature, the artist spent most of his childhood tracking creatures great and small across the rocky ridgelines and wooded mountainsides, perfecting his tracking skills and keen ability to spot what many of us never see. It was once said that the artist could identify approaching hummingbirds from two counties away with one eye, while tracking a fast-moving, bouncing black bear on a pogo stick with the other eye.

Despite his many accomplishments, his most important discovery and skill is the ability to spot the deceptive BigFoot that walks among us but remains unseen by most. After spending decades learning the habits of this elusive, mythical creature, the tracker/artist has finally agreed to share his journals that capture the sightings of the infamous, larger-than-life creature that has mystified generations.

Now you have the opportunity to sharpen your search-and-find skills by finding not only BigFoot and his legendary footprint, but also the many other unusual and sometimes unexpected people, creatures, and objects that can be found at anytime . . . anywhere.

Happy Searching!